JULIE B. HUGHES

Running Into Poetry

An invitation to be present on your path

First published by Run to Write 2022

Copyright © 2022 by Julie B. Hughes

All rights reserved. No part of this publication may be reproduced, stored or transmitted in any form or by any means, electronic, mechanical, photocopying, recording, scanning, or otherwise without written permission from the publisher. It is illegal to copy this book, post it to a website, or distribute it by any other means without permission.

Julie B. Hughes asserts the moral right to be identified as the author of this work.

Julie B. Hughes has no responsibility for the persistence or accuracy of URLs for external or third-party Internet Websites referred to in this publication and does not guarantee that any content on such Websites is, or will remain, accurate or appropriate.

Front cover photo: by Lena Gadanski from Getty Images via Canva.com

About Author page photo: Alice G Patterson @alice@agpphoto.com

First edition

ISBN: 9781737690704

This book was professionally typeset on Reedsy. Find out more at reedsy.com

*To my running and writing buddies all over the world.
Thank you.*

Contents

A Note to the Reader:	iv
SUPERPOWER	1
YOU AND THE ROAD	3
DO YOU RUN?	4
WHAT IT TAKES	6
ONWARD	7
ENCHANTED RUNNER	8
COLORFUL STRIDE	9
RUN LOVE	10
AUTUMN TUNNEL	11
RUNNING ON FAITH	12
MUD of LIFE	13
HINT FROM THE WIND	15
GAINING	16
BE THE STREAM	17
ORANGE MOON	18
ROLLICK RUN	19
CATCH AND CHASE	20
SQUASH STRESS	21
PONYTAIL SWAY	22
FESTIVE RUN	23
I WILL RUN	24
HEALING TRAIL	25
MAGIC RUN	26

RUNNING IS...	27
LEAN IN	28
SNOW WHISPERS	29
RUN TO WRITE	30
WIDE OPEN TRAIL	31
DON'T GIVE UP	32
RECESS RUN	33
HILLS TO TACKLE	34
RUN FOR COFFEE	35
WORDS CAPTURE	37
SOLITARY RUNNER	38
60-MINUTE RUN	39
EYES ON THE GOAL	41
STEP INTO NATURE	42
FOX	43
BOUND UPHILL	45
WINS	46
RUN BUDDY	48
I WILL NOT BACK DOWN	49
COAST	51
FIRST BRIGHT SPOT	52
RESILIENT TREE	54
SHOW UP	55
NEW YEAR'S RUN	56
BELIEVE IN YOU	57
TRUST THE ROAD	58
MOTHER RUNNER	59
BLUEBIRD	60
TRY AGAIN	61
4:30 A.M.	62
MORNING RITUAL	63

WEARY RUNNER	64
A NEW PATH	65
ANOTHER MOTHER RUNNER	66
I RAN TODAY	67
SUPERHERO	69
SHADOW	70
RUNNER WRITER	72
FREE	73
BREATHE IN LOVE	74
About the Author	75

A Note to the Reader:

These poems were created during and after runs. They were influenced during a season of tremendous challenge for my family. Running and writing helped me cope during these moments of sadness, loss, joy, and love. Many of the poems you will read are from this moment. A moment when I was working hard to stay optimistic and not let my negative thinking consume me. Whichever path you may be on, my hope is these poems will remind you of the beauty, hope, love, and joy all around you when you seek for it— when you deliberately look for it.

"May Running Into Poetry become your soundtrack to show up, encourage, and cheer you on your path." -julie b. hughes

SUPERPOWER

We mother runners
    Cherish our time on the road
    Power in our legs

The miles are fuel
    A charge, freedom in our minds
    Fire in our hearts

Energy we need
    Motherhood we can handle
    Purple toenails too

Let go of the guilt
    Run, a moms superpower
    Keep pushing courage

We are enough moms
    Remind yourself this each day

Be yourself, believe

We will do hard things
    Running is one we embrace
    Bring it on, *Let's go!*

YOU AND THE ROAD

Lace-up your sneakers
   No responsibility
   You and the road, free

DO YOU RUN?

Do you run?
   Is it to prove something
   to someone
   Is it to beat someone
   or something
   Is it to escape

Do you run?
   Is it for a certain time?
   To maintain a pace
   To log the miles
   Do you run?
   Alone on the trail
   Be with your thoughts
   Nature to awaken you
   Solitude

Do you run?
   Yes, I do
   Run to forget
   Run to be free
   Run to let go

DO YOU RUN?

Run to be me
Mind and body
Heart and breath
I run to connect it all
I do run
It's when I like myself the best

WHAT IT TAKES

The weather changes
   Keep showing up on the road
   Lean forward, lean in

You will make it mom
   The climb is sometimes long-yet
   You have what it takes

ONWARD

Whatever lies ahead
   You're running the race
   You build endurance
   Resilience and strength

In the miles you run
   In the challenges you face
   Through the peaks and valleys
   Keep your pace

Onward and upward!
   You shout
   The attitude to have
   No doubt

ENCHANTED RUNNER

Outdoor runs refresh her soul
    Connected to nature makes her whole
    Wonder and miracles all around
    Her feet barely touching the ground
    Magical pavement
    A carpet ride
    Her senses come alive
    Trees draped with snow
    Branches outstretched wide
    Welcome enchanted runner
    we are your guide.

Chimney smoke clings to the air
    Pine needles peek out of the snow—Stare
    Winter birds singing above
    Her heart permeates with love
    Appreciation for her body and mind
    God's wonderful design

COLORFUL STRIDE

Running in the fall
   The leaves covering the road
   Red, orange, yellow stride

RUN LOVE

Running with the breeze
   This is the time I seize
   The sunshine on my face
   Grateful for the pace
   The leaves on the ground
   Crunch under my feet-
   This weather can't be beat
   The fall colors I spot
   Love is what I got

AUTUMN TUNNEL

A tunnel of color
   on her right and left
   She hears the rustling of leaves
   the sound of her breath

The autumn season she loves
   A great time to run
   Enjoying the miles
   before the season is done

She knows winter will come
   Embracing the change
   The squeaky of the white ground
   Leaves for snow exchange

RUNNING ON FAITH

Faith to keep going
   Pray, run, be still with Jesus
   God's courage to thank

My gift to embrace
   I didn't stop believing
   Friend and Good Shepard

MUD of LIFE

Bound up the trail of life
   Peer around the bend
   Leap over rocks and roots
   Your legs in pursuit
   Zig zag the turns
   Mud puddles appear

How deep is the bottom?
   Will I get sucked in?
   My sneakers will get wet
   I'm not sure I'm ready yet.

Questions spin
   yet you must keep your pace
   No time to stop—
   Keep on moving
   Even if you face-plant
   don't say you can't

You're still in the race

One big adventure
Time to embrace
the mud and mess of life
It's what brings us to
the other side.

HINT FROM THE WIND

The wind pushes against her
   She leans forward
   and pushes right back
   Swinging her arms with
   a little more power
   Shortening her stride
   and fighting back.

The wind stays steady
   She keeps her pace
   Hang on just a bit longer
   Relief is around the corner
   The wind now at her back
   Propelling her forward
   She feels light on her feet
   Like nothing can stop her
   The wind to thank for this reminder—

 She is capable
   She is strong
   The wind will come and go
   Yet she will carry on.

GAINING

Get out the door, run!
   Gaining ground in the morning
   The best time of day

BE THE STREAM

Rolling over rocks
    Finds a way around the bend
    Pushing through the leaves
    Gentle yet mighty
    Keeps flowing, continues on
    Be the stream, bounce on.

—*Be the stream, Bounce on*

ORANGE MOON

Upward towards the sky
    What a sight! *Moon, is that you?*
    I pick up the pace
    Morning run adventure, chase
    Exhilarating orange moon

ROLLICK RUN

Rain hits rat-a-tat
   Sneakers are wet and heavy
   Splash in the puddles

Trail dark pitapat
   Frolic, kick around drip-drop
   Morning rollick run

CATCH AND CHASE

Trail runs in the fall
    Leaves running ahead to catch
    Amusing to chase

SQUASH STRESS

Squash the stress
   Wrestle down the worry
   Anxious thoughts race
   Action plan in place
   Walk or run
   Pray or dance
   No right or wrong
   You get the chance

Opportunity to take charge
   Pen in hand
   Watch out thoughts
   I know where I stand
   I can handle any emotion that comes up
   A thought to repeat
   A tool I use that can't be beat.

PONYTAIL SWAY

Her ponytail sways
   Side to side, her eyes ablaze
   Enthusiasm for the road
   A time, place to let it all go
   Both feet are off the ground
   Look!
   She is flying now
   Drop the should, would, could
   It's all good!
   Let the ponytail sway
   It's her time to play

FESTIVE RUN

Sweet refreshing smell
   Conifers in the forest
   Festive winter run

I WILL RUN

The weather will change, will do what it does
I will run.
The weather will howl and scream
I will run.
The weather will throw down rain and snow
I will run.
The weather will try to deter me yet
I will run.
The weather will make my mind work hard
I will run.
The weather will make me second guess
I will run.
The weather will build my resilience
I will run.
The weather is part of the adventure
I will run.
The weather I will embrace—*I will run.*

HEALING TRAIL

Living trees gather
   Minty scent is her shelter
   Unshakeable roots
   Run the trail was her breakthrough
   Nature to soften her pain

MAGIC RUN

Snow globe magic run
   Snowflakes swirl together hug
   Runner's secret joy

RUNNING IS...

Running is solitude
   Running is space
   Running is breathe, relax
   Keep my pace

Running is to fly
   Running is free
   Running is uphill and down
   A time to be me

Running is conversation
   Running is play
   Running is joy and love
   Fresh air, yay!
   —*Running is...*

LEAN IN

I confront the hill
   Lean in, legs and arms obey
   I am a runner
   Dynamic body and mind
   I flow on the road and grin

SNOW WHISPERS

Outside for a run
   The snow whispers to the ground
   My breath forms a cloud

RUN TO WRITE

Thoughts on paper
  Thoughts on the road
  Both a time to create
  Or let it all go

Out on the road
  Then over the paper
  Space to be free
  And time to savor

A moment of clarity
  The "aha" we all want
  Now a sentence to share
  To spread love and care

WIDE OPEN TRAIL

The wide open trail
   Tall trees -refreshing blue sky
   Is my happy place

DON'T GIVE UP

Cross the finish is the goal
    Your legs are burning
    Your body wants to quit
    Your mind starts to grumble
    Is the finish line here yet?

You hear the cheers
    You can do it!
    Don't give up now
    You have what it takes
    You got the know-how

Bring a good attitude
    Mental toughness you will need
    Leave your self-doubt at the door
    You will finish—*glow evermore!*

RECESS RUN

Run is my playtime
   Trees, sun, road my companions
   Nature diversion

HILLS TO TACKLE

I tackle the hill
   Lean - leap into the crisp air
   I am flying now
   Light on my feet floating high
   I glide on the road and grin

RUN FOR COFFEE

Run for coffee
   That's how we roll
   To keep the legs moving
   Cold wind blows
   When the air is frozen
   Our eyelashes too
   Run for coffee
   Is our view
   Bound along snowy roads
   Faces covered, eyes peek out
   FIVE MORE MILES we shout!

Run for coffee
   A cuppa Joe each
   Fuels us to keep pushing
   We are almost in reach
   Strong aroma
   Bold taste on our tongues
   Warms our body and soul
   Run to Skytop coffee is our goal
   We embrace all weather
   Rain, wind, or snow

Coffee is the motivation—
A long run treat, celebration.

WORDS CAPTURE

Words keep coming
   On the page
   In hopes, they do engage
   To spread love and encouragement is the goal
   She pushes through the hesitation
   Dreams the words inspire, bring resonation

On the road is when the words blow in
   Bouncing around with every stride
   The miles alive, her guide
   Open-eyed sentences fill her head
   Do they matter
   There is so much chatter

Sharp, aware she makes the run home
   Write them down, empty her mind
   For tomorrow a new day, a new run
   And more words to come

SOLITARY RUNNER

It's dark and quiet
   Snow falls on my eyelashes
   Solitary now
   Fog forming with each exhale
   I delight the loneliness

60-MINUTE RUN

60-minute run
   What will I see today
   When I look up instead
   Keep my eyes ahead- a hawk
   Glides, wings outstretched soars
   I fly alongside the trees

A woodpecker to my right
   What a sight
   Bright red hanging out on a tree
   Look up Julie so much to see
   Keep looking up
   Snow packed trails beneath
   The firm ground reassures me
   Look around as you pump your arms
   Look around as you pick up the pace
   My sneakers firmly laced

Breathing the cold crisp air
   Awakens my soul
   Self-connection is the goal
   I know where I'm going

I know who I am
—*I am...*

EYES ON THE GOAL

I have what it takes
    Bring it on mother nature
    I can handle it
    The weather I can't control
    I keep my eyes on the goal

STEP INTO NATURE

Redwing blackbirds sing
   Water shimmers by the trail
   Mud grabs my sneakers

FOX

I lookup
   Just in time
   A red bushy tail
   Darts in front of my eyes
   A fox!
   Sprints onto the road
   I follow her footprints in the snow
   Chase or being chased- I don't know

I pick up the pace
   To catch up with her
   My competitive spirit ignites
   I'm chasing with no fright
   My eyes fixed
   On the fox ahead
   Look at her run
   Oh! What fun
   Where is she going
   It's still snowing

She disappears into the woods
   I lose her tail, the red is gone

The chase has ended
My run adventure splendid
This is what the outdoors can do
You never know
Who you will run into

BOUND UPHILL

We bound up the hill
   Into the bold morning sky
   Mighty in our minds
   A pink hue lit up the path
   Let us rejoice and be glad

WINS

Look for the small wins
   I tell myself each day
   To keep going and bring
   Happiness-is my way
   The laundry folded and put away
   The dishes aren't done
   That's okay
   Look for the wins is all I say

A healthy homemade meal
   is what I'm proud of
   I moved my body a run outside
   I kept my mind on the upside
   I will be deliberate with the wins
   My brain needs the practice
   It can act like a cactus
   Prickly and sharp
   I don't want the negative to take heart

I will focus on the triumphs
   Though small they maybe
   It matters to the brain, you see

WINS

Stay optimistic
Keep cheering yourself on
Look for the wins
You got this! Press on.

RUN BUDDY

Conversation, run
   It's not about pace just, run
   Movement nature, run
   Fresh air to fill us up, run
   Awaken our senses, run

I WILL NOT BACK DOWN

The wind is fierce
   As she begins her climb
   Lean forward, head down
   Arms pump to get her knees up
   She shortens her stride

The hill is the obstacle
   She needs to confront
   No way around it but up
   You could turn around
   Begins the conversation
   Resign to the elevation
   You don't need to climb this hill
   Turn around, aren't you feeling ill?

The thoughts zoom in
   But she is ready–
   I will climb this hill
   Strong and steady
   I will not back down
   I will keep pushing

My legs are strong
   My mind is too
   I will repeat these thoughts
   I know what is true
   I will get up this hill
   My mind is in control
   I will make it to the top
   —I will not stop

COAST

I coast down the road
   Into the wide open air
   I am free floating
   Without the pressure to please
   I run relaxed and carefree

FIRST BRIGHT SPOT

Light vest flashing bright
   Hat with a light
   Reflective vest with phone
   Flashlight on, I'm in the zone
   I got all the lights so I glow
   A 50-minute run in the dark, Go!
   Roads clear though snow is coming
   No matter, my mind-body humming
   I'm alert to cars as they pass
   In and out of driveways fast
   Gas stations, stop signs
   Do they even see me shine?

A truck speeds out of the lot
   doesn't bother to spot
   Me running on the side
   He zooms out in his ride
   I'm flashing light as I run
   Can't they see me I'm like the sun
   Oh well must have somewhere to be
   I keep my eyes alert on the road- see
   A snowplow rumbles past

FIRST BRIGHT SPOT

Gives a beep beep blast
I give a wave fast
I'm noticed at last!

RESILIENT TREE

Wind aggressive, fierce
    Rock the trees, branches wave swing–
    Laced my sneakers though
    My mind says *go back to bed*
    I'm like a tree- resilient

Wind will make me strong
    This sentence gets me outdoors
    Build mental toughness
    I want to do hard things, run
    I'm like a tree- resilient

SHOW UP

The road and a pair of sneakers is it run
    Step out into the cold crisp air commit run

Ground beneath, the sky above wide-open, run
    Space to swing arms, pump legs no time to sit run

Longer the distance the more connected, run
    The mind, body, and heart show up don't quit, run

Runner enjoys the solitude, calm, peace run
    Miles of road stretched out ahead builds grit run

The road I love no matter the weather, run
    I thank God for this gift, it keeps me fit run

NEW YEAR'S RUN

90-minutes of road
    On the first day of 2022
    It's exactly what I want to do
    Lace-up the sneakers
    Throw on my vest
    My body and mind will take care of the rest

Meet up with a run buddy
    Reflect on how far we've come
    Running to the beat of our own drum
    Go us! Press on
    Persistence, courage, grit
    We won't quit

Our run goals are ready
    Our attitude is set
    Watch out 2022—
    You haven't seen nothing yet!

BELIEVE IN YOU

Believe in yourself
   It's really that simple
   It doesn't need to be complicated
   Though the whispers linger
   Those mumbles are musty
   Stale and uninspired
   An old story on the shelf
   Time to let go—I say

Leave it there let it collect dust
   You get to write a new story, *you must*
   Take the leap
   Deep inside your ready
   You know what you're meant to do
   Go for it!
   I'm cheering for you.
   —*You can do it!*

TRUST THE ROAD

There are several roads to travel
   Which one do you take?
   Stay small, stay quiet, hide your light
   Straight forward, fewer turns, and climbs—
   Don't go looking for change
   Yet a feeling was rising
   This road didn't seem right
   Curiosity grew and courage too
   To stop the cycle, a choice to make
   Face the fears, let failure be—
   There is nothing wrong you see
   Shine your light as you make the climb
   Some sharp turns, jagged ledges you will find
   Push against the status quo
   Seems to be the way to grow
   Trust the road shining your light
   It will lead to great things—
   The adventure in life

MOTHER RUNNER

Rise early to get out the door mother runner
    Alone under the dark sky no other runner

Silence in the morning clears the mind-breath runner
    Time to feel free energized not smother runner

Snow whispers to the ground wake up feet crunch runner
    Eyes wide snowplow up ahead oh brother runner

Dash across the road avoid the plow, safe runner
    Adventure awaits here comes another runner

A wave, good morning smile stride along runner
    Julie, it will be a great day mother runner

BLUEBIRD

I hear *tu-a-wee, tu-a-wee*
   Ears alert to the soft sound
   Eyes dart to the trees and all around
   Tu-a-wee as I run past
   Eyes smile to see
   A bluebird on a branch

TRY AGAIN

Try again
   First, second, third time
   Try again
   And you will find
   Lessons learned, growth, and progress
   Failures will happen
   It's all part of the process

Try again
   It will happen this time
   Press on, pivot
   You got this climb
   Try again
   Trust and believe
   You have what it takes
   You will succeed!
   —*Go on, try again...*

4:30 A.M.

4:30 a.m. training run
    She's up before the sun
    Rise and shine out of bed
    Pulls a hat over her head

Fresh, brisk air hits her face
    Down the road at her pace
    Snow flattened on the ground
    Her sneakers crump with every bound

Music to her ears
    Imagining the sounds are cheers
    Enthusiasm and energy bubble through her veins
    Her imagination used to soften her pains

MORNING RITUAL

Alarm beeps in the dark morning
   I can hear the outside, pouring
   I'm up for a run
   My day has begun
   Out the door for some exploring

WEARY RUNNER

Weary runner
   Some days are hard
   Climbs are long
   Legs feel heavy
   You look up to mountains
   Whisper
   Where is the valley?

A downhill would be nice
   Or at least an easier path
   The rocks, elevation, and turns difficult
   You're not sure how long you will last

Yet you've faced challenges before
   And made it through
   Believe in yourself
   You will make it to the summit soon

Keep fighting back
   Don't back down
   One step at a time
   Is your new mantra now

A NEW PATH

Hilly climbs surround you
   Challenges you need to face
   The only way is up
   Gulp
   Do I have what it takes

Can I handle this detour?
   It came out of the blue
   Do I embrace this new path
   Or dig my heels in and stew

You can do this
   I hear a voice
   Yes you have what it takes
   Accept the road you're on
   One small step
   I know you can take

Keep pushing courage
   Grab my hand
   Keep your eyes and heart open
   In your weakness— He has a plan

ANOTHER MOTHER RUNNER

There was a mother of two kids
   She wanted ten arms like those squids
   To finish the chores
   Then be out the doors
   Oh! what a sight for the eyelids

I RAN TODAY

I ran today
   Three simple words
   I ran today

My way to shine light
   Today's all right
   Bird song in the air
   Ponytail sways without a care
   I ran today
   My energy is up
   Coffee in my cup
   Breakfast varies
   Oatmeal, banana, and berries
   I ran today

Thankful for my food
   Blessed with my mood
   Gratitude for the miles
   Appreciation and smiles
   I ran today
   High five to you
   If you ran too

It's all good
We ran today!

SUPERHERO

You cross the finish
   A superhero feeling
   You are strong, brave, bold
   Nothing is impossible
   Two thumbs up mother runner

SHADOW

Four-degree winter run
    Thank you, Lord for the bright sun
    Her shadow comes out to play
    She's been hiding
    You hope she stays

A dark silhouette impossible to lose
    She's running in your shoes—
    Out in front pumping her arms
    Muscular and brave
    Her ponytail sways

The light shines just right
    A charge—
    Power to run—
    Ignite
    You try to catch up
    Run alongside
    Your stride always just one step behind

You keep on running
    She does too

SHADOW

Of course
The shadow is you
—*Embrace your shadow too*

RUNNER WRITER

There once was a runner writer
    Who thought her poems made running brighter
    To rhyme was such fun
    Silly laughs each run
    Her pen, sneakers made life lighter

FREE

I feel secure, free
   Wide open spaces
   Nothing can stop me
   Gain ground on the roads
   I feel at home

Ready to fly
   A bird soaring high
   Forward motion
   Beats the commotion
   Fresh air even if it's cold
   I am bold

BREATHE IN LOVE

Long run Saturday
   Morning runaway
   Legs charge down the road
   Self-care to unload

Empty the thoughts with every stride
   God will take them captive- your guide
   Trust Him in all you do
   The spirit lives inside of you

Breathe in love
   Exhale fear
   Your faith is the anchor
   You will make it my dear

About the Author

Julie B. Hughes shares her love of running through poetry in her third book. She lives with her husband Jeff, and two children Brindsley and Delaney in Manlius, NY. She is the author of My Road: A Runner's Journey Through Persistent Pain to Healing and Run to Boston: Poems for the Marathoner.

You can connect with me on:
- https://juliebhughes.substack.com
- https://facebook.com/juliebhughes

Subscribe to my newsletter:
- https://juliebhughes.substack.com

www.ingramcontent.com/pod-product-compliance
Lightning Source LLC
Chambersburg PA
CBHW051643130526
44590CB00068B/2818